Teddy Bear, Teddy Bear

A CLASSIC ACTION RHYME

Illustrated by
MICHAEL HAGUE

Morrow Junior Books
NEW YORK

Printed in the United States of America.

1 3 5 7 9 10 8 6 4 2

Library of Congress Cataloging-in-Publication Data
Hague, Michael.
Teddy bear, teddy bear / illustrated by Michael Hague.
p. cm.
Summary: An illustrated version of the traditional rhyme that
follows the activities of a teddy bear.
ISBN 0-688-10671-4—ISBN 0-688-12085-7 (library)
1. Nursery rhymes. 2. Children's poetry. [1. Teddy bears—Poetry.
2. Nursery rhymes.] I. Title.
PZ8.3.H11935Te 1993
398.8—dc20 92-17997 CIP AC

Watercolors and pen and ink were used for the full-color art.
The text type is 40 pt. Lionel.

Book design by Marc Cheshire

To Kirk, Earlene, Kevin, and Taylor Ann

Teddy Bear,
Teddy Bear,
turn around.

Teddy Bear, Teddy Bear, touch the ground.

Teddy Bear, Teddy Bear, show your shoe.

Teddy Bear, Teddy Bear, that will do!

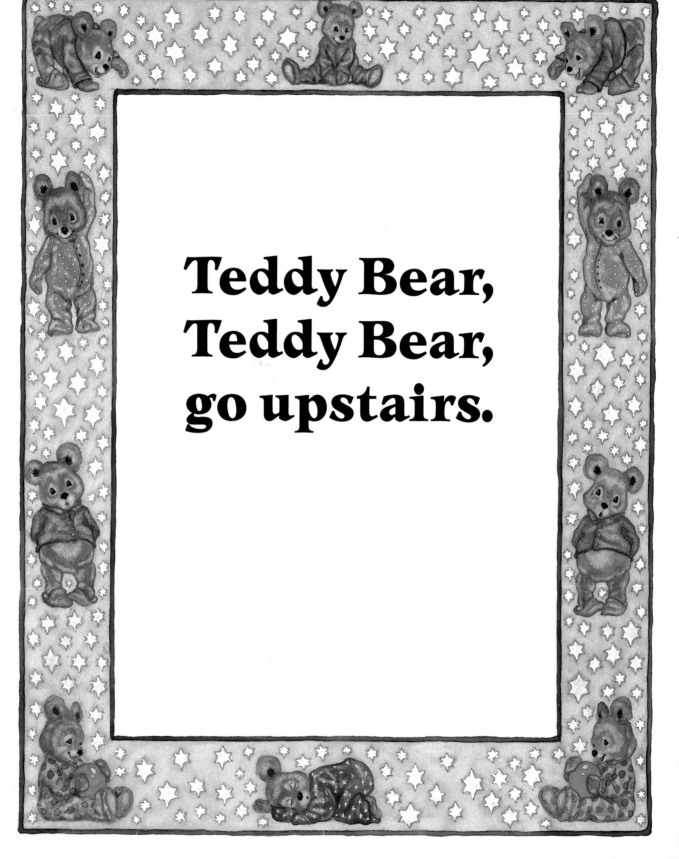

Teddy Bear,
Teddy Bear,
go upstairs.

Teddy Bear, Teddy Bear, say your prayers.

**Teddy Bear,
Teddy Bear,
turn off
the light.**

Note to Parents

"Teddy Bear, Teddy Bear" is an action rhyme that you and your child can act out together. As you read the rhyme, you should perform the actions described below as your child follows along.

Teddy Bear, Teddy Bear, turn around.
Spin around once.

Teddy Bear, Teddy Bear, touch the ground.
Bend your knees and touch the floor.

Teddy Bear, Teddy Bear, show your shoe.
Lift your foot and point to your shoe.

Teddy Bear, Teddy Bear, that will do!
Bow dramatically.

Teddy Bear, Teddy Bear, go upstairs.
Pretend to walk upstairs.

Teddy Bear, Teddy Bear, say your prayers.
Put your hands together and bow your head.

Teddy Bear, Teddy Bear, turn off the light.
Lift your arm and pull an imaginary cord.

Teddy Bear, Teddy Bear, say good night.
Put your hands together and place them next to your cheek.

About the Artist

Michael Hague is the artist of *Alphabears* and *Numbears*, two best-selling bear books written by his wife, Kathleen. In addition, he has illustrated nearly twenty children's classics, including *Twinkle, Twinkle, Little Star*, *The Wind in the Willows*, *Alice's Adventures in Wonderland*, *Peter Pan*, *The Velveteen Rabbit*, and *The Secret Garden*.

"I tend to approach most books in a similar fashion. First, I make some small compositional sketches, which for me is always the most important step. These small thumbnails are then enlarged to full-size sketches on watercolor boards, where I develop the details of the pictures. After the pencil illustrations are complete, I'm ready to begin painting. I put a neutral wash of color over the entire board with a wide brush. When the wash has dried, I begin to paint the details in watercolor. Only after coloring everything do I go in with my ink lines, colored pencils, and airbrush.

"The wonderful childhood rhyme *Teddy Bear, Teddy Bear* suggested to me that I try something different with my style of painting. By combining a realistic bear with stylized, brightly colored backgrounds, I think a magical fantasy world has been achieved."

Mr. Hague lives in Colorado Springs, Colorado, with his wife and their three children.